Worship

The Global Hallelujah!

Worship
The Global Hallelujah!

Edited by Barbara Colborn
Designed by Jewel Fink

Wycliffe
BIBLE TRANSLATORS

Wycliffe Bible Translators USA, Orlando, Florida 32862.
© 2000 by Wycliffe Bible Translators.
All rights reserved. Published 2000.
Printed in the United States of America.

ISBN 0-938978-19-5

Acknowledgments for other text and photos appear at the end of this book.

*W*orship—*The Global Hallelujah!* was created by Wycliffe Bible Translators USA to bring glory to God and to bring context to the purpose of missions. Our desire is to reflect His glory through sharing and participating in worship around the world.

We look forward to the day when people of every nation, tribe and language will worship before God's throne. He has given us the privilege of being part of this plan to bring the nations to Himself. We believe that God's Word in the heart languages of the world's peoples is essential to evangelism, Christian growth and discipleship.

Wycliffe is committed to Vision 2025—seeing Bible translation in progress for every language group that needs it by 2025. This is a vision for the whole church. More than 3,000 language groups still need the Word in their language. To find out how you can help meet this need, contact us at:

Wycliffe
BIBLE TRANSLATORS

P.O. Box 628200
Orlando, FL 32862-8200
1-800-WYCLIFFE
www.wycliffe.org

The Global Hallelujah!—the whole world praising God! God calls all peoples to Him. They come in need, in prayer, in song—in His strength, for His glory.

No one language is enough to describe Him. But as we envision people from every language, every culture, every part of the world coming to God, we glimpse something of His greatness and His great love. And as God's people around the world come before Him in worship, we glimpse God's character and creativity reflected in their faces, actions and offerings.

Stock./Corbis

After this I looked and there before me was a great multitude that no one could count, from every nation, tribe, people and language, standing before the throne and in front of the Lamb. They were wearing white robes and were holding palm branches in their hands. And they cried out in a loud voice: "Salvation belongs to our God, who sits on the throne, and to the Lamb.

Revelation 7:9 (NIV)

what we were created for

Thailand/Photo by Craig Duddles

Worship is:

what we were created for.

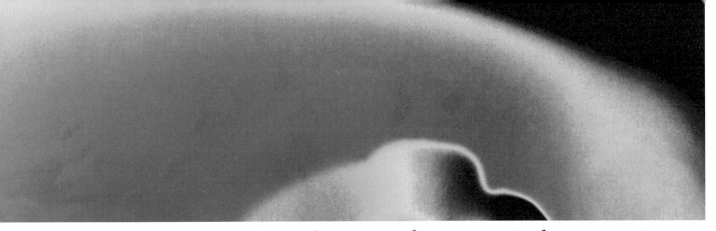

"He is the God who made the world and everything in it. Since he is the Lord of heaven and earth, he doesn't live in man-made temples, and human hands can't serve his needs—for he has no needs.

He himself gives life and breath to everything,

and he satisfies every need there is. From one man he created all nations throughout the whole earth. He decided beforehand which should rise and fall, and he determined their boundaries.

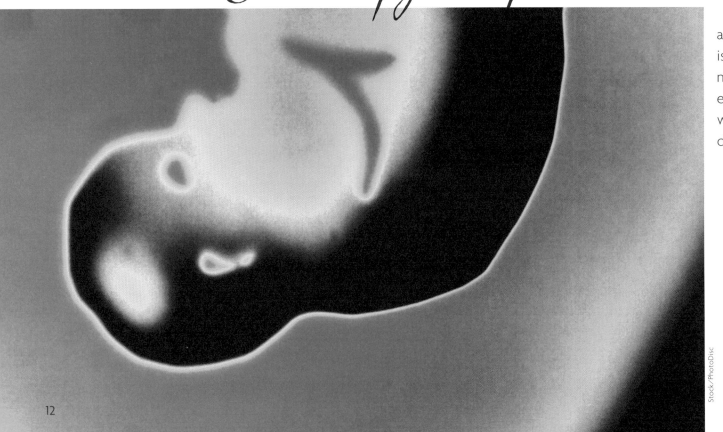

His purpose in all this was that the nations should seek after God and perhaps feel their way toward him and find him—though he is not far from any one of us. For in him we live and move and exist. As one of your own poets says, 'We are his offspring.' And since this is true, we shouldn't think of God as an idol designed by craftsmen from gold or silver or stone. God overlooked people's former ignorance about these things, but now he commands everyone everywhere to turn away from idols and turn to him. For he has set a day for judging the world with justice by the man he has appointed, and he proved to everyone who this is by raising him from the dead."

Acts 17:24–31 (NLT)

South Asia/Photo by Dean Schauer

Worship is: *acknowledging our Creator.*

O LORD God Almighty, who is like you? You are mighty, O LORD, and your faithfulness surrounds you. When its waves mount up, you still them. ...The heavens are yours, and yours also the earth; you founded the world and all that is in it.

Psalm 89:8,9,11 (NIV)

Shout for joy to the LORD, all the earth, burst into jubilant song with music; make music to the LORD with the harp, with the harp and the sound of singing, with trumpets and the blast of the ram's horn—shout for joy before the LORD, the King.

Psalm 98:4–6 (NIV)

In one sense, God doesn't need our worship. He doesn't need our praise, affirmation, or congratulations. He doesn't need our worship any more than He needs our food, our money, or our service. He is totally complete without us! However, as far as His saving purpose for our lives is concerned, He has chosen to ask for our worship. Worship is an essential part of His plan. As we give Him honor, He puts us in a position that enables us to know and enjoy His goodness. What love! God asks to be given something that benefits us! His "need" is nothing more than His means of bringing us to Himself.

—Martin R. DeHaan II

Worship is what we were created for.
This is the final end of all existence: the worship of God.

—John Piper

Worship is: *praising God just as He created us.*

Well, folks, we praise the Lord, we lift up His name. We are happy with Jesus, we Saramaccans.

Master Jesus has come to us Saramaccans. He has taken us just the way we are. He has given us His love, just the way we are. We serve Him just as we are, we Saramaccans.

We are dressed in the Saramaccan way, we men in our loincloths, the ladies in their skirts. We've been dancing in our ways. We Saramaccans rejoice and God isn't angry with us. He is not taking offense. He's very happy with us. He's been waiting a long time for people like us to praise Him in this way, with all our hearts.

Suriname/Photo by Bob Mantell

16

Don't you know what God's Word says? It says we should praise Him with all our strength—with all our hearts, with all our might—just as we are.

He is very happy with our manner of praising Him, because we're not pretending to be something we're not. We are genuine.

You don't have to be afraid that if you become a Christian you have to stop expressing happiness the way we express our happiness. No! God takes us just the way we are. You don't have to stop being Saramaccan if you follow Master Jesus.

In worship we can come before Him, just as we are...because of who He is.

—Saramaccan leader

Suriname/Photo by Bob Mantell

Jesus takes me just the way I am. That means...

_____
_____
_____
_____
_____
_____
_____
_____
_____
_____
_____
_____
_____
_____
_____
_____
_____
_____
_____
_____
_____
_____

Worship is: *God's children gathering to proclaim His faithfulness.*

...you are a chosen people, a royal priesthood, a holy nation, a people belonging to God, that you may declare the praises of him who called you out of darkness into his wonderful light.

1 Peter 2:9 (NIV)

Papua New Guinea/Photo by Brian Reese

Gathering together is an important means of encouraging one another to persevere in love and obedience. As we expose ourselves to the ministries of others and to the Word of God, we are encouraged to engage with God as the family of God together.

—*David Peterson*

Chile/Photo by Jim Rupp

Theologian Justo Gonzalez describes Hispanic Christian worship as a fiesta. "It is a celebration of the mighty deeds of God. It is a get-together of the family of God."

—Nathan Corbitt

Churches in the San Martín Quechua culture of Peru gather for an annual music festival. The church chosen to sponsor the music festival for the coming year sets aside a field for growing crops. Everyone works together in the field to bring in extra cash and grow crops that will be used to feed the many visitors. The women commit themselves to raising an agreed-upon number of chickens, pigs or other animals, and to making new clay soup bowls. The men commit to fishing and hunting. As the time for the festival approaches, the women choose a site for the communal kitchen and go to neighboring churches to ask for assistance in cooking for the four-day festival. Everyone helps by bringing the needed firewood. A growing number of musical groups write new hymns throughout the year to be presented at the festival.

—People of Peru

Golin./Papua New Guinea/Photo by Don Hesse

A childlike heart enjoys time alone with a father, giving full attention and receiving full attention. Jesus constantly was getting away to be alone with the Father—even while the masses were trying to get to Him.

—*Darrell Evans*

We do not only worship God because He is the Creator, but because He is "Daddy," the loving Head of our household who we follow. We worship Him out of relationship. The God we worship is also the "Father of our Lord Jesus Christ" (Ephesians 1:3). That means that you cannot worship God if you leave out Christ.

—*Tony Evans*

Kaugel/Papua New Guinea/Photo by Robert Head

Stock/Photo Disc

As a child of God, I want to show Him I love Him by...

_____

_____

_____

_____

_____

_____

_____

_____

_____

_____

_____

_____

_____

_____

_____

_____

_____

_____

_____

_____

_____

_____

_____

_____

In Europe many generations ago, the dear old saint of God, Brother Lawrence, was on his deathbed. Rapidly losing his physical strength, he witnessed to those gathered around him: "I am not dying, I am just doing what I have been doing for the past forty years, and doing what I expect to be doing for all eternity!"

"What is that?" he was asked. He replied quickly, *"I am worshiping the God I love!"*

Worshiping God—that was primary for Brother Lawrence. He was also dying, but that was secondary. He knew why he had been born again.

Yes, and Brother Lawrence is still worshiping God. He died and they buried his body somewhere, but his was a living soul, created in the image of God. So, he is still worshiping with all the saints around the throne of God.

—A.W. Tozer

Worship is: *both quiet trusting and loud proclaiming.*

A visitor to one church in southern Sudan—a church that meets under a very large tree—reported: "The most amazing part of their gatherings is watching the lavish worship of these people of God. As the service ends the people have a meal together. After the meal the worship continues. These believers are not ashamed to sing and praise God at the top of their voices as they walk for a mile through their town, witnessing to their great love for Jesus."

—*Ray Thorne*

Chiang Mai, Thailand. It's 6 p.m. and worshipers are beginning to gather for evening worship. Flower gardens and lawns provide a serene and welcome setting at the Seven Flowers Seminary. The wood frame building is void of chairs; only mats provide a place to sit. Worshipers gather on the mats and then take a reflective and silent cross-legged position—in complete silence.... One of the participants takes a small acoustic guitar and gently strums a few chords of introduction as worshipers quietly chant a unison chorus in the Thai language.

—*Nathan Corbitt*

Because true worship brings us to God, worship pleases Him. He takes pleasure in any attitude of heart that bows low or lifts us up in appreciation of His matchless wonder.

—*Martin R. DeHaan II*

True worship takes time, and one of the evidences that we are starting to make spiritual progress in our worship is the calmness that comes to the soul as you wait before God. You are conscious of time but not controlled by time. You enjoy waiting before the Lord and reveling in His wonder and His greatness.

—*Warren Wiersbe*

Find rest, O my soul, in God alone; my hope comes from him.

Psalm 62:5 (NIV)

Ethiopia/Photo by Dean Schauer

Worship is: *the flow of God's Spirit through lives of those who depend on Him.*

Sabaot/Kenya/Photo by June Hathersmith

Sabaot/Kenya/Photo by June Hathersmith

Yet a time is coming and has now come when the true worshipers will worship the Father in spirit and truth, for they are the kind of worshipers the Father seeks. God is spirit, and his worshipers must worship in spirit and in truth.

John 4:23,24 (NIV)

...worship is a response—an active, open, unguarded response to God, whereby we declare His worth in an intimate manner, leaving Him room to touch us, to flood us with His peaceful presence.

—Charles R. Swindoll

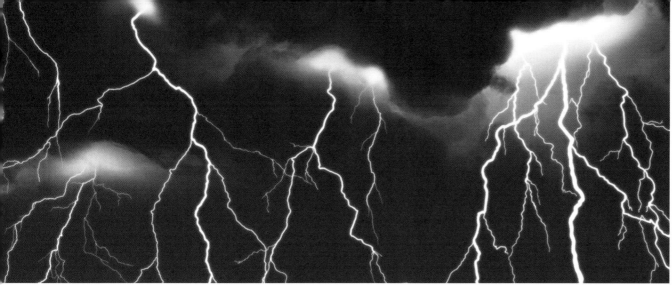

Stock/Photo Disc

Vital worship relates men to God, the source of power, that through man his power may be made manifest.

—Gaines S. Dobbins

Blessed be God, blessed be God forever,
Who in time and eternity lives;
God, the Lord who loves justice and mercy
And who heals and forgives those who fall.
God will bandage the wounds of the broken,
And pay heed to each body and soul;
God has asked humankind not to fear
But to believe that the kingdom's at hand.

—song from the Philippines by Salvador T. Martinez

I have seen God reveal His power by...

_____
_____
_____
_____
_____
_____
_____
_____
_____
_____
_____
_____
_____
_____
_____
_____
_____
_____
_____
_____
_____
_____
_____
_____
_____
_____

25

On the flanks of Mount Ewati, an extinct volcanic uplift in Uganda, there is a valley. I had always wanted to drive closer to that valley, as it looked so unique. So when I found there was a road that passes right through the heart of the volcanic lands, I tried it.

The scenery was inspiring. Great striped cliffs rose here and there, topped by unruly mops of trees twisting their way out over empty space in their quest for sunlight. Ancient spatter cones rose like the ruins of some great pyramid, now covered with the rubble of scrubby brush and burnt rock. And above it all stood the soaring peak of Ewati, its topmost crags seeming to hang from the sky itself.

On one occasion, when I was transporting a group of young African musicians back to town from the village where we lived, I turned off the truck road to take this "scenic route." At first the young folk were hesitant. This was not the fastest way, and it

Democratic Republic of Congo/Photo by June Hathersmith

Spain/Photo by Craig Duddles

went through the territory of a different clan than they were used to dealing with. But one of the young men allayed their anxiety and began to tell the story of when his father had come to this valley on an evangelistic crusade many years before.

Five pastors had organized for an inspirational speaker to come and break new ground. But alas, for the first four days, no one would listen. Instead, the men and youth of the villages openly mocked the pastors, pelting them with drunken slurs, ribald remarks, and on occasions, stones. The women and girls flatly refused to listen, instead they fled, lest they be punished by their men folk for encouraging the outsiders. Each night was spent praying fervently that God would break down the walls of darkness and open the hearts of these stubborn, proud people. But it seemed to no avail.

Finally, on the fifth and last day of the crusade, the speaker turned to the spectacular scenery. In a voice quavering with anguish for the lost, he cried out to the rocks, the trees and the sacred mountains themselves to break forth in joyous praise for their Creator, whom the residents of that valley had refused to acknowledge. Then the pastors fell to their knees and all began praising the Lord as each knew how.

The response of the people was immediate and dramatic. By droves, overcome by the urging of the Holy Spirit and cut to the core by the challenge of the evangelist, they came down to pray and accept Jesus as their Lord and Savior.

By the time the young man had finished his story, the vehicle was quiet. I felt a lump the size of Ewati itself building in my throat. Just

27

then, as if to dramatize the moment, the road reached the saddle overlooking the valley. Golden beams of light shone through a patchwork of backlit clouds illuminating and emulsing the panorama with a golden light, as if Heaven itself had opened a window to shine on this particular spot.

I stopped the car to relish the sight. Then without prompting, one of the girls began to sing, "All hail the power of Jesus' name, let angels prostrate fall. Bring forth the golden di-i-i-a-adem and crown Him Lo-ord of all...." The rest of the worship team joined her in a full-fledged, joyous, unbridled worship for the Creator and Lord of the universe.

I cannot drive that route, or even pass that valley, without lifting up my praise to God. And when I hear the song, "All Hail the Power of Jesus' Name," my mind is filled with the memory of the valley of Ewati and the promise that someday the hills and rifts of the area we worked in would also echo with praise for the Creator as its residents turned from their confusion to worship the one true God in purity and holiness.

—*Jack Shoemaker*

Kenya/Photo by June Hathersmith

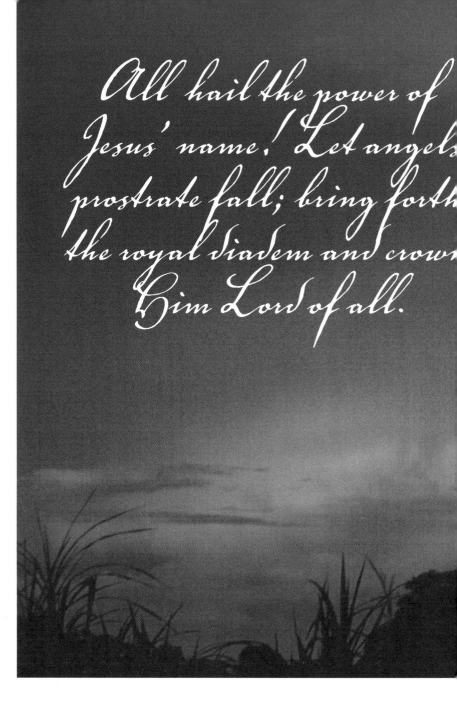

All hail the power of Jesus' name! Let angels prostrate fall; bring forth the royal diadem and crown Him Lord of all.

Africa/Photo by Craig Duddles

A time when I just couldn't contain my praise for God was...

_____
_____
_____
_____
_____
_____
_____
_____
_____
_____
_____
_____
_____
_____
_____
_____
_____
_____
_____
_____
_____

30 Peru/Photo by Craig Duddles

30

Worship is:

listening to God and taking Him to heart.

"The farmer sows the word.

Some people are like seed along the path, where the word is sown. As soon as they hear it, Satan comes and takes away the word that was sown in them. Others, like seed sown on rocky places, hear the word and at once receive it with joy. But since they have no root, they last only a short time. When trouble or persecution comes because of the word, they quickly fall away.

Choctaw/Mississippi/Photo by Craig Duddles

Binukid/Philippines/Wycliffe Photo Files

Still others, like seed sown among thorns, hear the word; but the worries of this life, the deceitfulness of wealth and the desires for others things come and choke the word, making it unfruitful. Others, like seed sown on good soil, hear the word, accept it, and produce a crop—thirty, sixty or even a hundred times what was sown."

Mark 4:14–20 (NIV)

The first time the seed of God's Word started growing in me was...

_____

_____

_____

_____

_____

_____

_____

_____

_____

_____

_____

_____

_____

_____

_____

_____

_____

_____

_____

_____

_____

_____

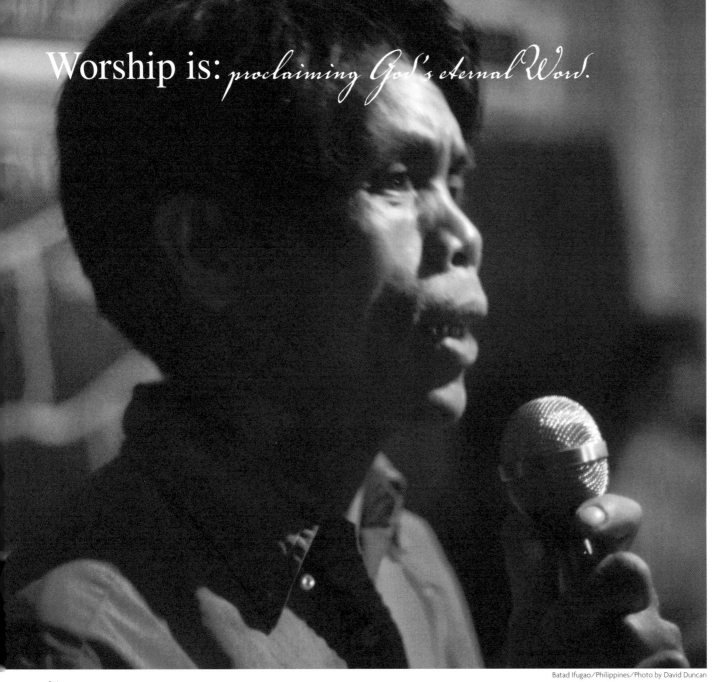

Worship is: *proclaiming God's eternal Word.*

Preaching is worship. It is the heralding of good news about God in Christ by a person who is called, sent and anointed by God to make Biblical truth plain, beautiful and powerful.

—*John Piper*

...at its best, preaching is itself an act of congregational participation in which the hearts of the people rise in adoration or confession or thanksgiving as the words of the preacher become in Calvin's phrase, "the voice of God resounding in them."

—*Paul Lewis*

We worship God only to the degree that we hear Him speak. This is why there are injunctions throughout Scripture about hearing and listening.

—*R.T. Kendall*

Batad Ifugao/Philippines/Photo by David Duncan

Wycliffe Photo Files

Father God really loving all people sent his only son from the sky to where the people are in order to die. They believing will not suffer, but will live with him.

John 3:16 (English paraphrase of Yora translation, Peru)

The Word may come through preaching and teaching, through personal witness in word or song, or through study and meditation; but it always comes (if we are receptive) with that power to renew us. This is why the believer must spend time daily with the Bible, reading and meditating; and why the Word must be an important part of public worship.

—Warren Wiersbe

Mexico/Photo by Hugh Steven

Worship is: *letting the light of God's Word into our lives.*

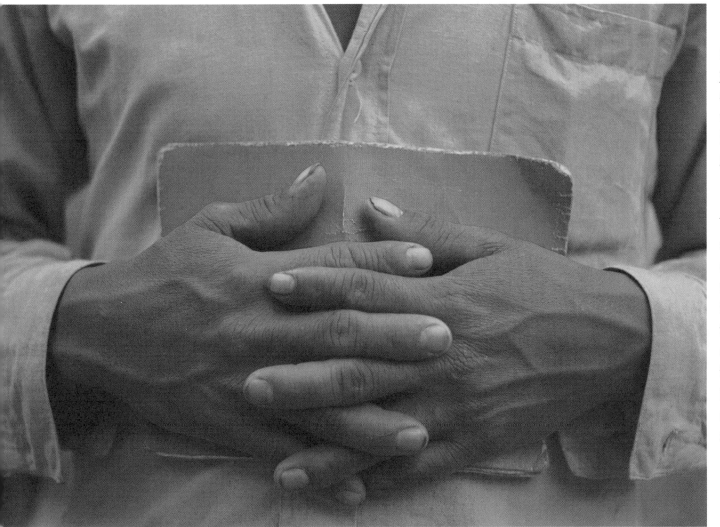

Chile/Photo by Hugh Steven

Let the word of Christ dwell in you richly as you teach and admonish each other with all wisdom, and as you sing psalms, hymns and spiritual songs with gratitude in your hearts to God.

Colossians 3:16 (NIV)

To "let the word dwell richly" means to pursue the word eagerly, to receive it gladly, to meditate on it regularly, to obey it unswervingly, to cling to it tenaciously, to share it enthusiastically, and to cherish it faithfully. The richness of our life in the word overflows in the singing of psalms and hymns and spiritual songs.

—*Bruce H. Leafblad*

Each person in the congregation must think for himself or herself and assess whether what the preacher is saying is true or not. But if we listen with a defensive, aggressive, or spiteful attitude, then we will quench the Spirit before He can even speak.

—*R.T. Kendall*

The Father's Word is Word with heart.
We will receive it well and put it inside us
and stand as men.
The Father's Word is Word with nutrition.
We will receive it well and put it inside us
and stand as men.

—*Yawu church song, Papua New Guinea*

Ethiopia/Photo by Dean Schauer

A Scripture that really changed me is...

_____
_____
_____
_____
_____
_____
_____
_____
_____
_____
_____
_____
_____
_____
_____
_____
_____
_____
_____
_____
_____
_____
_____

Worship is: *welcoming God to change us.*

Mexico/Wycliffe Photo Files

True worship can only take place when we agree to God sitting not only on his throne in the centre of the universe but on the throne that stands in the centre of our heart.

—Robert Coleman

From the cowardice that dares not face new truth, from the laziness that is contented with half-truth, from the arrogance that thinks it knows all truth, Good Lord, deliver me. Amen.

—prayer from Kenya

I will give you a new heart and put a new spirit in you; I will remove from you your heart of stone and give you a heart of flesh.

Ezekiel 36:26 (NIV)

Behold, Lord, an empty vessel that needs to be filled. My Lord, fill it. My faith is weak; strengthen me. I am cold in love; warm me and make me fervent that my love may go out to my neighbor. I do not have a strong and firm faith; at times I doubt and am unable to trust you altogether. O Lord, help me. Strengthen my faith and trust in you....

—from a prayer by Martin Luther (1483–1546)

"Come now, let us reason together," says the LORD. "Though your sins are like scarlet, they shall be as white as snow; though they are red as crimson, they shall be like wool."

Isaiah 1:18 (NIV)

We please Him most, not by frantically trying to make ourselves look good, but by throwing ourselves into His arms with all our imperfections and believing that He understands everything—and loves us still.

—A.W. Tozer

Worship is: *surrendering our will to God's will.*

May the words of my mouth and the meditations of my heart be pleasing in your sight, O LORD, my Rock and my Redeemer.

Psalm 19:14 (NIV)

In Peru, a Sharanahua chief was helping translate the book of Acts. In the account of the lie told by Ananias and Sapphira, it tells us Peter said: "What made you do such a thing? You have not lied to men but to God." The Scriptures go on to report that when Ananias heard this, he fell down and died.

The chief grasped the meaning of the story. "Stop!" he said. "I have to pray." And he began to confess his secret sins to God.

This has now become a pattern for the Sharanahua people: that which is done in secret is confessed in secret, and that which is done openly is confessed openly.

—People of Peru

Jesus said to Peter..."Do you not know that my Father has commanded that I should suffer? And how can I say 'no' to Him?"

John 18:11 (English paraphrase of Muinane translation, Colombia)

What does God require? The answer is quite simple, and yet so deeply profound—self-surrender. This is the joyful exchange of an egocentric, sinful self for a God-centered self made whole. It is in fact a swap—our life for his and his life for us.

—*Robert Coleman*

With God's grace, I will stop saying "no" to Him about...

_____
_____
_____
_____
_____
_____
_____
_____
_____
_____
_____
_____
_____
_____
_____
_____
_____
_____
_____
_____
_____
_____
_____
_____
_____
_____

Worship is: *acknowledging God for who He is.*

"To whom will you compare me? Or who is my equal?" says the Holy One. Lift your eyes and look to the heavens: Who created all these? He who brings out the starry host one by one, and calls them each by name. Because of his great power and mighty strength, not one of them is missing.

Isaiah 40:25,26 (NIV)

To worship is to draw aside the veil between time and eternity, so we can see life in its eternal perspective.

—*James L. Christensen*

This is the paradox of Christian worship; we seek to see the invisible, know the unknowable, comprehend the incomprehensible, and experience the eternal.

—*Warren Wiersbe*

Worship is a human response to a divine revelation. God has said something, and I respond to it. God is doing things, and I respond to them. On occasion, the appropriate response may be absolute silence as we meditate on our God. On other occasions, the best response may be the loudest possible voice of praise.

—*Charles R. Swindoll*

You are God, you have great power
You have raised the dead
You have opened the ears of the deaf
And the eyes of the blind
You have spoken to the waters and they obeyed
You have spoken to the evil spirits and they were humbled
You are God
You are God

—*Ife song, Togo*

expressing our love to God

Budu/Democratic Republic of Congo/Photo by June Hathersmith

Worship is:

expressing our love to God.

One of the Pharisees asked Jesus to come to his home for a meal, so Jesus accepted the invitation and sat down to eat. A certain immoral woman heard he was there and brought a beautiful jar filled with expensive perfume. Then she knelt behind him at his feet, weeping. Her tears fell on his feet, and she wiped them off with her hair. Then she kept kissing his feet and putting perfume on them.

When the Pharisee who was the host saw what was happening and who the woman was, he said to himself, "This proves that Jesus is no prophet. If God had really sent him, he would know what kind of woman is touching him. She's a sinner!"

Then Jesus spoke up and answered his thoughts. "Simon," he said to the Pharisee, "I have something to say to you."

"All right, Teacher," Simon replied, "go ahead."

Then Jesus told him this story: "A man loaned money to two people—five hundred pieces of silver to one and fifty pieces to the other. But neither of them could repay him, so he kindly forgave them both, canceling their debts. Who do you suppose loved him more after that?"

Simon answered, "I suppose the one for whom he canceled the larger debt."

Stock/Photo Disc

"That's right," Jesus said. Then he turned to the woman and said to Simon, "Look at this woman kneeling here. When I entered your home, you didn't offer me water to wash the dust from my feet, but she has washed them with her tears and wiped them with her hair. You didn't give me a kiss of greeting, but she has kissed my feet again and again from the time I first came in. You neglected the courtesy of olive oil to anoint my head, but she has anointed my feet with rare perfume. I tell you, her sins—and they are many—have been forgiven, so she has shown me much love. But a person who is forgiven little shows only little love." Then Jesus said to the woman, "Your sins are forgiven."

The men at the table said among themselves, "Who does this man think he is, going around forgiving sins?"

And Jesus said to the woman,

"Your faith has saved you; go in peace." Luke 7:36–50 (NLT)

If I knew Jesus was going to come to my house for dinner tonight, I'd...

_____

_____

_____

_____

_____

_____

_____

_____

_____

_____

_____

_____

_____

_____

_____

_____

_____

_____

_____

_____

_____

_____

Worship is: *a heart that sings to God.*

Our heart, our desire,
is to see the nations worship.
Our cry, our prayer,
is to sing Your praise to the ends of the earth.
That with one mighty voice
every tribe and tongue rejoices.
Our heart, our desire,
is to see the nations worship you.

—American song by John Chisum and George Searcy
(© 1993, Integrity Music, Inc.)

Budu/Democratic Republic of Congo/Photo by June Hathersmith

Singing is the Christian's way of saying: God is so great that thinking will not suffice, there must be deep feeling; and talking will not suffice, there must be singing.

—*John Piper*

God doesn't expect us all to have great voices. He doesn't care how well we can carry a tune—and some of us couldn't carry a tune in a bucket! But God sees the heart, and the melody is there.

—*R.T. Kendall*

In one country where believers have been persecuted for their faith, believers meet in small, secret prayer services. In case anyone overhears them singing, their hymns have been set to the tunes of political propaganda songs.

—*Global Worship Report*

You turned my wailing into dancing...

You turned my wailing into dancing; you removed my sackcloth and clothed me with joy, that my heart may sing to you and not be silent. O Lord my God, I will give you thanks forever.

Psalm 30:11,12 (NIV)

Father God, the things you created,
the things you created are exceedingly many.
We are seeing them, we are receiving them and thanking you.
Praise, praise, beautiful Father God.

—Yawu song, Papua New Guinea

In 1994 there was a spiritual awakening amongst the Yawu people and many began to compose songs that the Holy Spirit gave to them. The songs were taught to others after the Yawu church leaders approved of them. Even children came forward with new songs. These Christian songs followed the traditional music patterns and were also accompanied by the log drums, an awesome sound. The Yawu people often sing these songs

Yawu/Papua New Guinea/Photo by Helen Marten

from dusk to dawn, especially as they are preparing for Christmas. They sing with joy and enthusiasm. Some of the new songs are accompanied by guitars and are sung in the church services, which are held three times a week.

—Helen Marten

...each generation of Christians carries with it its contemporary songs and sounds that reiterate the continuing theme of God's grace. As they are passed on to new generations, they leave the legacy of the power of God to continually redeem the culture and to reveal the timeless truths of the gospel.

—Daniel Benedict and Craig Kennet Miller

Here's my song to God:

_____
_____
_____
_____
_____
_____
_____
_____
_____
_____
_____
_____
_____
_____
_____
_____
_____
_____
_____
_____
_____
_____

Worship is: *both a personal experience and a shared experience.*

If worship is a decision, then the greatest worship happens when someone who doesn't like a church's music or liturgical style prays, "Not my will but yours be done, God—I'll worship you in spite of it."

—*Geoff Bullock*

...God means for us to hear each other pray and sing so that there can be corporate responses of agreement—Amen.

—*John Piper*

Let us not give up meeting together, as some are in the habit of doing, but let us encourage one another—and all the more as you see the Day approaching.

Hebrews 10:24 (NIV)

52

Bless the Lord, O my soul;
And all that is within me,
bless His holy name.

Psalms 103:1 (NKJV)

The Scriptures speak of God rejoicing over his children with singing (Zephaniah 3:17). At one level, those who are graciously saved respond to the Savior with song. Meanwhile, the all-gracious and eternally saving Father sings over those who are singing to him. What this divine singing is like no one can imagine. It is as unfathomable and irresistible as grace itself. It springs out of grace, it is driven by redeeming love and consummated in the victory of Christ, and it results in the songs with which the church graces its praise.

—Harold Best

Papua New Guinea / Photo by Perry Schlie

Worship is: *proclaiming the victory of Christ in the midst of difficulties.*

Have you ever wondered how Paul and Silas could sing praises in a Philippian jail after being stripped, flogged and clamped in the stocks? Or how Jesus could sing a hymn on the eve of his arrest, knowing everything that was about to happen to him? Or how Paul could describe worship with the spine-tingling phrase "living sacrifice"? It was because their worship was not based on what they liked. It was based on who they loved.

Worship is not a result of how good the music is or whether my favorite songs are sung. It is not a consequence of whether I stand or sit, lift my hands or kneel. My worship must be an expression of my relationship with God—in song, in shouts and whispers, sitting, walking or driving the car. Worship is my response to God.

—Geoff Bullock

Comitancillo/Guatemala./Photo Edgar Stephen Beach

The Bible says that Jesus Christ "appeared for this purpose, that He might destroy the works of the devil" (1 John 3:8). When your spiritual adversary shows up, if you will turn to Christ in worship and get Him on the case, you might see more things finished more quickly.

This aspect of worship is very meaningful to the African-American community. We witnessed this way of dealing with our enemies in the march to Selma, on the steps of the statehouse in Montgomery, Alabama, and in cities all across the Deep South.

When the authorities came, perpetrating a system of ungodliness, the marchers went to their knees. They sang and prayed, and the federal government sent troops to protect the freedom marchers. Every time they came up against a dog, a billy club, or a hate-filled person, they got down on their knees and prayed. They worshiped.

The reason I can eat anywhere is that men got on their knees and worshiped. Worship changed the laws of the land.

—*Tony Evans*

Shout for joy, O heavens; rejoice, O earth; burst into song, O mountains! For the Lord comforts his people and will have compassion on his afflicted ones.

Isaiah 49:13 (NIV)

Worship is: *honoring Jesus Christ as the source of our life.*

In the New Testament Jesus Christ is the great Worshiper in his obedience, priesthood and offering, summing up the old and modeling the new worship of God. He once for all offered himself for us, an unblemished and uniquely suitable sacrifice for sin. This was his unique and supreme act of worship, and it calls forth from us a response to his finished work in terms both of celebration and dedication.

—Paul Lewis

The Lord's Supper is worship because it expresses the infinite worth of Christ. No one is more worthy to be remembered and no one is more worthy to be proclaimed. And no one can nourish our souls with eternal life but Christ. So let us come and remember, and proclaim and eat.

—John Piper

Burrar/Australia/Photo by Paul Smith

Nyaboa/Cote D'Ivoire/Photo by June Hathersmith

56

"*This is my body, given for you; do this in remembrance of me.*" Luke 22:19 (NIV)

Nyaboa/Cote D'Ivoire/Photo by June Hathersmith

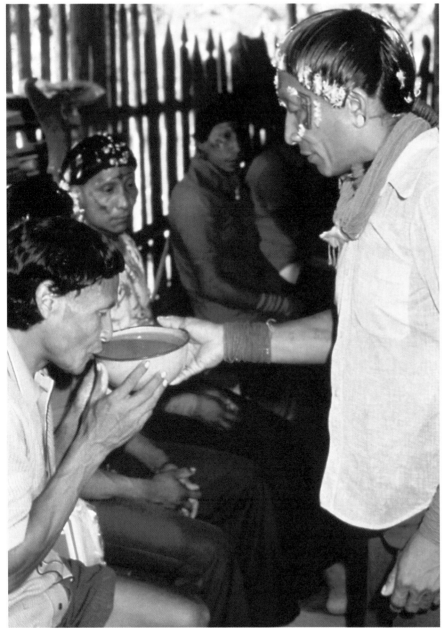

Hixka/Brazil/Wycliffe Photo Files

...all who take these common elements into their bodies are inviting Christ to be formed in them and to touch every cell of their lives as this bread and wine will go to every cell of their bodies.

—*Howard W. Roberts*

There are some Christians who receive the sacramental elements in a standing position, thus symbolizing the majesty of God in whose presence they stand to attention. Others there are who receive the sacramental bread and wine sitting at a table, this position signifying the friendly hospitality of the omnipotent God. The communicants are guests at his table. And then there are the Christians who kneel to receive the bread and wine in an attitude of humility before God, the God who dwells with those "who are of a humble and contrite heart." Three different attitudes—standing to salute the majesty of God, sitting to share the fellowship of God, kneeling in humility before the infinite compassion of God. These differences in observance serve to enlarge and enrich our conception and experience of God.

—*Ralph W. Sockman*

"Love so amazing, so divine,
Demands my soul, my life, my all."

Help us each, gracious God, to live in such magnanimity and restraint that the Head of the church may never have cause to say to any one of us, "This is my body, broken by you." Amen
—*prayer from China*

_____
_____
_____
_____
_____
_____
_____
_____
_____
_____
_____
_____
_____
_____
_____
_____
_____
_____
_____
_____
_____
_____
_____
_____
_____
_____

Hixka/Brazil/Wycliffe Photo Files

Sabaot/Kenya/Photo by June Hathersmith

Worship is:
living to please God.

Worship is: *giving our lives as a testimony to His life.*

...you were buried with Christ when you were baptized. And with him you were raised to a new life because you trusted the mighty power of God, who raised Christ from the dead.

Colossians 2:12 (NLT)

Baptism confirms that people recognize God's love, acceptance and approval of them before they ever do anything. It really does signify the end of the search to belong.

—*Howard W. Roberts*

Baptism has become a symbolic way of saying, "I am ready to grow. I willingly entrust myself to God's creative power to grow me beyond where I am."

—*Howard W. Roberts*

Christian worship is offering....we are invited to offer ourselves to God. Through our lives God possesses new entrances into the world, and through the offering of our lives to God true worship occurs.

—*Tim and Jan Wright*

As the triumphal entry of Jesus into Jerusalem indicates, there is a time for love to overflow in elation, exhibition, enthusiasm, and excitement, but the most important quality in worship's love is obedience.

— *Judson Cornwall*

Budu/Democratic Republic of Congo/Photo by June Hathersmith

Worship is: *living in the love of God and living out the love of God.*

"...love each other in the same way that I love you. And here is how to measure it—the greatest love is shown when people lay down their lives for their friends."

John 15:12,13 (THE MESSAGE)

Stock/Photo Disc

Worship can turn duty into love and merely good works into a thing of beauty.

—Ben Patterson

I cleaned houses in college as a business. One in particular stands out in my mind. It was my first day at the house and we went over the usual "here is this, here is that" routine. Then my "client" rocked me back on my heels. She simply said, "Sean, I just want you to honor God with the way you clean my house. The rest will take care of itself." Honor God? This was toilets and dusting, not fasting and prayer. But I learned what she meant. I didn't cut corners. I did unexpected things I wasn't asked to. I honored God.

—Sean Womack

For me to express my love for my wife Janine, I must do more than say "I love you." I must mow the lawn, pick up my socks, wash the car, share her dreams and visions and goals—I must be a partner to her, working to be a team that expresses mutual love to each other selflessly. In this I discover that the best intimacy forces you to get up in the morning after making love with your wife the night before and go and mow the lawn, fix the kitchen door, paint the shed—to do things that are produced out of love.

It's the same in our relationship with God. I can't sing, "I love you, Lord," "I'll worship you," "Be exalted," without being a partner in his will and vision.

Of course we must sing and dance and praise the Lord. But if while we sing and dance and praise we either ignore God's commission or create a culture that alienates those whom God has called us to reach, are we really worshiping God at all? Or are we worshiping the worship instead of him?

—Geoff Bullock

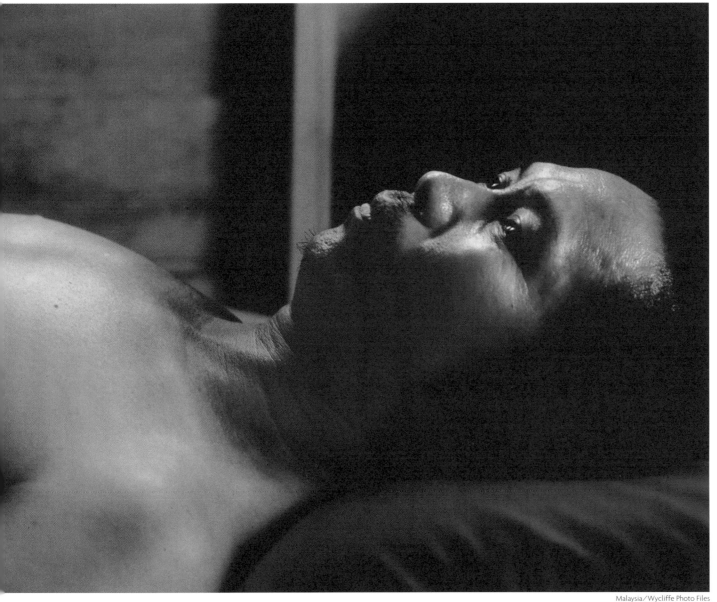

Malaysia/Wycliffe Photo Files

One day an expert in religious law stood up to test Jesus by asking him this question: "Teacher, what must I do to receive eternal life?"

Jesus replied, "What does the law of Moses say? How do you read it?"

The man answered, "'You must love the Lord your God with all your heart, all your soul, all your strength, and all your mind.' And, 'Love your neighbor as yourself.'"

"Right!" Jesus told him. "Do this and you will live!"

The man wanted to justify his actions, so he asked Jesus, "And who is my neighbor?"

Jesus replied with an illustration: "A Jewish man was traveling on a trip from Jerusalem to Jericho, and he was attacked by bandits. They stripped him of his clothes and money, beat him up, and left him half dead beside the road.

"By chance, a Jewish priest came along; but when he saw the man lying there, he crossed to the other side of the road and passed him by. A Temple assistant walked over and looked at him lying there, but he also passed by on the other side.

"Then a despised Samaritan came along, and when he saw the man, he felt deep pity. Kneeling beside him, the Samaritan soothed his wounds with medicine and bandaged them. Then he put the man on his own donkey and took him to an inn, where he took care of him. The next day he handed the innkeeper two pieces of silver and told him to take care of the man. 'If his bill runs higher than that,' he said, 'I'll pay the difference the next time I am here.'

"Now which of these three would you say was a neighbor to the man who was attacked by bandits?" Jesus asked.

Ethiopia/Photo by Craig Duddles

The man replied, "The one who showed him mercy."

Then Jesus said,

"Yes, now go and do the same."

Luke 10:25–37 (NLT)

God, I want to love You by yielding to You and letting You love people through me, people such as...

_____
_____
_____
_____
_____
_____
_____
_____
_____
_____
_____
_____
_____
_____
_____
_____
_____
_____
_____
_____
_____
_____
_____

Worship is: *admitting our need of God to God.*

O God, forgive me for my stupidity, my blindness in success, my lack of trust in Thee. Be Thou now my Savior in success. Save me from conceit. Save me from pettiness. Save me from myself! And take this success, I pray, and use it for Thy glory. In Thy strength, I pray. Amen.

—*Peter Marshall (1902–1949)*

To admit need to the Lord is an act of humility and worship, because the needy heart is really saying: "Lord, You are my only source; I believe You are 'I AM'—my all in all. No one can satisfy the longings of my heart like You can. I could never live without You."

—*Darrell Evans*

As the deer pants for streams of water,
so my soul pants for you, O God.

Psalm 42:1 (NIV)

God wants us just to look to Him and say, "Lord, I don't know how much I love you. But I know how much you love me." Rest on that and let God love you. Then you will stand in awe.

—R.T. Kendall

God is often silent when we prefer that he speak, and he interrupts us when we prefer that he stay silent. His ways are not our ways. To live with the sacred God of creation means that we conduct our lives with a God who does not explain himself to us. It means that we worship a God who is often mysterious—too mysterious to fit our formulas for better living.

—Craig Barnes

Ghana./Wycliffe Photo Files

69

Worship is: *offering ourselves to God.*

Everything comes from him;
Everything happens through him;
Everything ends up in him.
Always glory! Always praise!
  Yes. Yes. Yes.

So here's what I want you to do, God helping you: Take your
everyday, ordinary life—your sleeping, eating, going-to-work,
and walking-around life—and place it before God as an offering.
Embracing what God does for you is the best thing you can do for
him. Don't become so well-adjusted to your culture that you fit into
it without even thinking. Instead, fix your attention on God. You'll
be changed from the inside out. Readily recognize what he wants
from you, and quickly respond to it. Unlike the culture around you,
always dragging you down to its level of immaturity, God brings the
best out of you, develops well-formed maturity in you.

Romans 11:36–12:1,2 (THE MESSAGE)

Stock/Digital Stock

Ghana/Photo by Becky Keller

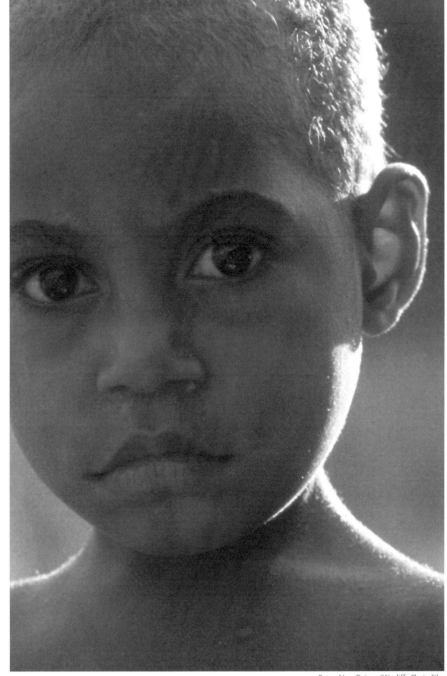

Humbly in Your sight we come together, Lord,
Grant us now the blessing of Your presence here,
These, our hearts, are Yours; we give them to You, Lord,
Purify our love to make it like Your own.

These, our eyes, are Yours; we give them to You, Lord,
May we always see Your world as with Your sight,
These, our hands, are Yours; we give them to You, Lord,
Give them strength and skill to do our work for You.

These, our feet, are Yours; we give them to You , Lord,
May we walk along the path of life with You,
These, our tongues, are Yours; we give them to You, Lord,
May we speak Your healing words of life and truth.

These, our ears, are Yours; we give them to You, Lord,
Open them to hear Your words of guidance, Lord,
Our whole selves are Yours; we give them to You, Lord,
Take us now and keep us Yours forevermore.

—Tumbuka song, Malawi, words by Tom Colvin
(© 1976, Hope Publishing Co.)

Worship is: *glorifying God all day, every day, in everything.*

And whatever you do or say, let it be as a representative of the Lord
Jesus, all the while giving thanks through him to God the Father.

Colossians 3:17 (NLT)

O Jesus, be the canoe that holds
me in the sea of life; be the steer
[rudder] that keeps me straight;
be the outrigger that supports
me in times of great temptation.
Let your Spirit be my sail that
carries me through each day.
Keep my body strong, so that I
can paddle steadfastly on,
in the long voyage of life.

—*prayer from New Hebrides*

Peru/Photo by Craig Duddles

A good path expresses a concept of worship among the Kiowa Native American people.... Indian people have a tradition of travel on very well-worn paths that laid the foundation for much of the highway system in the United States. Walking a good path implies a life free from anger, strife and prejudice. ...Many traditional Christian songs speak of personal experience on this good path. These people identify with the psalms because the metaphors of paths and journeys reflect their voice.

—Nathan Corbitt

Ifugao/Philippines/Photo by John Walton

Trust in the LORD with all your heart and lean not on your own understanding; in all your ways acknowledge him, and he will make your paths straight.

Proverbs 3:5–6 (NIV)

All of life is the outshining of what you truly value and cherish and treasure. Therefore all of life is worship. Either of God, or something else.

—John Piper

Ghana/Wycliffe Photo Files

the global hallelujah

Worship is:
the global hallelujah!

Shout for joy to the Lord, all the earth.

Worship the LORD with gladness;
come before him with joyful songs.
Know that the LORD is God.
It is he who made us, and we are his;
we are his people, the sheep of his pasture.

Enter his gates with thanksgiving
and his courts with praise;
give thanks to him and praise his name.
For the LORD is good and his love endures forever;
his faithfulness continues through all generations.

Psalm 100 (NIV)

"Give thanks to the LORD, call on his name; make known among the nations what he has done, and proclaim that his name is exalted.

Sing to the LORD, for he has done glorious things; let this be known to all the world."

Isaiah 12:4–5 (NIV)

Philippines/Photos by Don Hesse

Peru/Photo by Craig Duddles

77

Worship is: *praising God no matter where we are or who we are.*

Ghana/Photo by June Hathersmith

Whether you are five years old, or 50 or 90, God cares about your worship. He's not interested in your status in life. He looks at *you*.

—R.T. Kendall

...it is not how or when or with what degree of quality, variety, and imagination that we worship.

It is a passion about God that finds its voice.

—Howard Best

Suriname/Photos by Craig Duddles

Ethiopia/Photo by Dean Schauer

Papua New Guinea/Wycliffe Photo Files

Ethiopia/Photo by Craig Duddles

I have seen passionate worshipers in Indonesia and fervent tra-ditionalists in Northern Canada. From liturgical communities of faith in Oxford, England, to tribal communities in sub-Saharan Mali, God is doing great things in churches that appear to be incredibly different from one another. But are they truly different? Maybe truly great churches are not as different as they seem on the surface.

—R. James MacDonald

79

When we worship God, we will find Him far too wonderful to keep to ourselves.

—Martin R. DeHaan II

Peru/Wycliffe Photo Files

...witness is overheard worship. ...The specialists are usually called evangelists; the serendipitous are those whose worship is so ardent that they are prepared at any time or in any place to speak on behalf of the one they worship.

—*Harold Best*

Jesus is the way and the everlasting life.
Jesus is the owner of the truth.
If you want to go up to the Father,
come to Jesus and He will show you the way.

—*Vagla song, Ghana*

...worship can be expressed by sharing love with fellow believers, sharing the gospel with unbelievers, and meeting the needs of people on a very physical level. We can sum it up in a single word: acceptable worship is *giving*. It is a love that shares.

—*John MacArthur, Jr.*

In pressing us on to all the peoples, God is pressing us further into the humblest and deepest experience of his grace, and weaning us more and more from our ingrained pride. In doing this he's preparing for himself a people—from all the peoples—who will be able to worship him with free and white-hot admiration.

—*John Piper*

...witness is overheard worship.

Worship is: *the uniting of God's people to celebrate Him.*

God is not seeking worship in the abstract, but worshipers. The difference is significant. He seeks not only worshiping individuals, but a worshiping community, a universal community that worships the Lamb.

—*Felicity B. Houghton*

Here, O Lord, your servants gather,
Hand we link with hand,
Looking toward our Savior's cross,
 Joined in love we stand.
As we seek the realm of God, we unite to pray;
 Jesus, Savior, guide our steps, for you are the way.

Many are the tongues we speak, scattered are the lands,
Yet our hearts are one in God,
One in love's demands.
E'en in darkness hope appears,
Calling age and youth:
Jesus, teacher, dwell with us,
For you are Truth.

—*Japanese song, text by Tokuo Tamaguchi*
(© 1958, The United Methodist Publishing House)

Ghana /Photo by June Hathersmith

Komo/Democratic Republic of Congo/Photo by June Hathersmith

Fairest Lord Jesus, ruler of all nature,
O thou of God and man the Son,
Thee will I cherish, thee will I honor,
Thou, my soul's glory, joy, and crown!

Beautiful Savior! Lord of all the nations!
Son of God and Son of Man!
Glory and honor, praise, adoration,
Now and forevermore be thine!

—author unknown, possibly written
by Moravian Christians who fled Bohemia
in the eighteenth century

If at the end of my life God showed me what my worship of Him looked like, here is what I'd want to see:

_____
_____
_____
_____
_____
_____
_____
_____
_____
_____
_____
_____
_____
_____
_____
_____
_____
_____
_____
_____
_____
_____

Worship is: *the overflow of God's love to the whole world.*

... "*Peace be with you!*
As the Father has sent me, I am sending you."

John 20:21 (NIV)

Peru / Photo by Craig Duddles

Almighty God, look with compassion on all who are living
without you, and on the multitude who even in this land are
scattered like sheep without a
shepherd, or who in strange lands
are far from the church of their
fathers. Visit them with your
salvation. O heavenly Father, Lord
of the harvest, hear our prayers
and send forth workers into your
harvest. Fit and prepare them by
your grace for the work of their
ministry. Give them the spirit of
power, and of love, and of a
sound mind. Strengthen them to
endure hardness, and grant that
both by their life and doctrine
they may set forth your glory and
set forward the salvation of all
people; through Jesus Christ our
Lord. Amen.

*—adapted from the Prayer Book
of the Church of Ireland*

May our worship raise us up to know God, may it center on Jesus, and
may it point the way to the wedding feast of the Lamb. Then all our
worship will be "Amen!" and "Hallelujah!"

—Wayne Mueller

*God, I want to share Your love
with others around the world by...*

_____
_____
_____
_____
_____
_____
_____
_____
_____
_____
_____
_____
_____
_____
_____
_____
_____
_____
_____
_____
_____
_____

Worship is: *the weaving together of diverse people by one Spirit, one faith, to honor the one true God.*

During (a) time of worship a vision formed in my mind. I saw the earth as if viewed from space. Then hundreds of threads, each a different color, appeared from out of the nations, arcing out, upward and around the earth. As they met, they crisscrossed and weaved in and out of each other over the globe. With the multicolored threads still connected to their respective geographical starting points, a gigantic banner had been formed. It hung there billowing gently over the whole globe. I looked to see whether a design had emerged out of the weaving of the threads. On the underside, visible from the earth, was the face of Jesus. I knew immediately that the multicolored thread represented worship rising to the Lord from believers of every nation, people, tribe and language. The love gifts of millions of hearts lent color and distinctiveness by the contexts of vastly different cultures. This variety was the very thing that made the forming of the picture possible. —*Graham Kendrick*

When the flame of worship
burns with the heat of God's
true worth, the light of missions
will shine to the most remote
peoples on earth.

—John Piper

"All the earth shall worship You,
And shall sing praises to You;
They shall sing praises to Your
name."

Psalm 66:4 (NKJV)

As the people of God worship together, lifting their hearts to God
and experiencing His infinite blessing, their faces shine because
they're in His presence. That has an impact on the people of the
world that is impossible to measure. All our apologetics and evangelistic methods can never duplicate the impact of a true worshiper.

—John MacArthur, Jr.

..."Great and marvelous are your deeds, Lord God Almighty. Just and
true are your ways, King of the ages. Who will not fear you, O Lord,
and bring glory to your name? For you alone are holy. All nations will
come and worship before you, for your righteous acts have been
revealed."

Revelation 15:3–4 (NIV)

Authors and Sources of Information

Craig Barnes
When God Interrupts: Finding New Life Through Unwanted Change, (Downers Grove: InterVarsity Press, copyright © 1996). Used by permission; quoted on page 71.

Daniel Benedict and Craig Kennet Miller
Contemporary Worship for the 21st Century: Worship or Evangelism? (Nashville: Discipleship Resources, copyright © 1994). Used by permission; quoted on page 53.

Harold Best
Music Through The Eyes of Faith, The Christian College Coalition, copyright © 1993, (San Francisco: Harper). Used by permission; quoted on page 55, 83.

"Authentic Worship and Faithful Music Making," presented at the ACDA National Convention, February 27, 1999, copyright © 1999. Used by permission; quoted on page 80.

Geoff Bullock
"Beyond Self-Centred Worship," (Brisbane, Australia: *Renewal Journal,* www.pastornet.net.au/ renewal, copyright © 1995). Used by permission; quoted on page 54, 56, 67.

James L. Christensen
Don't Waste Your Time In Worship, (Grand Rapids: Baker Book House, copyright © 1978). Used by permission; quoted on page 45.

Robert Coleman
"Healing Through Worship and Healing in the Now," (Brisbane, Australia: *Renewal Journal,* www.pastornet.net.au/renewal, copyright © 1995). Used by permission; quoted on page 40, 43.

Nathan Corbitt
The Sound of the Harvest, (Grand Rapids: Baker Book House, copyright © 1998). Used by permission; quoted on page 21, 24, 75.

Judson Cornwall
Worship as Jesus Taught It, (Tulsa: Victory House Publishers, copyright © 1987). Used by permission; quoted on page 65.

Martin DeHaan II
What Kind of Worship Is God Looking For? (Grand Rapids: Radio Bible Class, copyright © 1987). Used by permission; quoted on page 17, 25, 82.

Gaines S. Dobbins
The Church at Worship, (Nashville: Broadman Press, copyright © 1962). Used by permission; quoted on page 27.

Darrell Evans
"A Childlike Heart in Worship," copyright © 1999, Darrell Evans, www.darrellevans.com. Used by permission; quoted on page 22, 70.

Tony Evans
What Matters Most, (Chicago: Moody Press, copyright © 1997). Used by permission; quoted on page 22, 57.

Global Worship Report, vol. 1, #1, "Creative Use of Secular Music," www.ad2000.org/ tracks/worship; used on page 51.

Felicity B. Houghton
"Some Reflections on the Meaning and Practice of Worship from Inside South America," *Worship: Adoration and Action,* D.A. Carson, ed., (Grand Rapids: Baker Book House, copyright © 1993). Used by permission; quoted on page 84.

R.T. Kendall
Before the Throne: A Comprehensive Guide to the Importance and Practice of Worship, (Nashville: Broadman & Holman, copyright © 1993). Used by permission; quoted on page 36, 39, 51, 71, 80.

Graham Kendrick
Public Praise, (Lake Mary, FL: Creation House, copyright © 1992). Used by permission; quoted on page 88.

Bruce Leafblad
"We'll Shout and Sing Hosanna," *Essays on Church Music in Honor of William J. Reynolds, School of Church Music,* copyright © 1998, Bruce Leafblad, (Fort Worth: Southwestern Baptist Theological Seminary). Used by permission; quoted on page 38.

Paul Lewis
"'Free Church' Worship in Britain," *Worship: Adoration and Action,* D.A. Carson, ed., World Evangelical Fellowship, (Grand Rapids: Baker Book House, copyright © 1993). Used by permission; quoted on page 36, 58.

John MacArthur, Jr.
The Ultimate Priority, (Chicago: Moody Press, copyright © 1983). Used by permission; quoted on page 83, 89.

R. James MacDonald.
"The Four Pillars," *Worship Leader,* www.worshipleader.org, copyright © 1998. Used by permission; quoted on page 81.

Helen Marten
Helen Martin, copyright © 1999. Used by permission; quoted on page 53.

Wayne Mueller
"Worship is Amen and Hallelujah!" a sermon presented at the opening service of the 1996 National Conference on Music, Worship and the Arts, Carthage College, Kenosha, Wisconsin. Entire sermon located on the Web site of Wisconsin Lutheran Synod (WELS) www.wels.net, copyright © 1996, Wayne Mueller. Used by permission; quoted on page 87.

Ben Patterson
Worship: Serving God with Our Praise, (Downers Grove: InterVarsity Press, copyright © 1994). Used by permission; quoted on page 66.

David Peterson
"Worship in the New Testament," *Worship: Adoration and Action,* D.A. Carson, ed., (Grand Rapids: Baker Book House, copyright © 1993). Used by permission; quoted on page 20.

People of Peru
Margarethe Sparing-Chávez, ed., (Lima: SIL, copyright © 1999). Used by permission; quoted on page 21, 42.

John Piper
From texts of sermons available at www.desiringgod.org, 1-888-346-4700. Used by permission.
"Worship God!" copyright 1997. Quoted on page 17.
"Amen, A Word Common to Many Cultures," copyright 1998. Quoted on page 36.
"Singing and Making Melody to the Lord," copyright 1997. Quoted on page 51, 54.
"The Lord's Supper as Worship," copyright 1997. Used by permission; quoted on page 58.
"All of Life as Worship," copyright 1997. Quoted on page 75.

Let the Nations Be Glad! (Grand Rapids: Baker Book House, copyright © 1993). Used by permission; quoted on page 83, 89.

Howard W. Roberts
Pastoral Care Through Worship, (Macon, GA: Smyth & Helwys Publishing, Inc., copyright © 1995). Used by permission; quoted on page 60, 64, 65.

Jack Shoemaker
Jack Shoemaker, copyright © 1999. Used by permission; quoted on page 28, 29, 30.

Ralph W. Sockman
Man's First Love, The Great Commandment, (New York: Doubleday, copyright © 1958). Used by permission; quoted on page 60.

Chuck Swindoll
Growing Deep in the Christian Life, copyright © 1986, 1995 by Charles R. Swindoll, Inc., (Grand Rapids: Zondervan Publishing House). Used by permission; quoted on page 26, 45.

Ray Thorne
Voice of the Martyrs, December 1998. (Bartlesville, OK: Voice of the Martyrs, copyright © 1998). Used by permission; quoted on page 24.

A.W. Tozer
Whatever Happened to Worship, compiled and edited by Gerald B. Smith, (Camp Hill, PA: Christian Publications, copyright © 1985). Used by permission; quoted on page 23, 41.

Warren Wiersbe
Real Worship, (Nashville: Baker Book House, copyright © 1986, 2000). Used by permission, quoted on page 25, 37, 45.

Saramaccan leader
Text translated from Saramaccan worship video, produced by SIL Vernacular Media, Suriname.

Sean Womack
"Work As Worship," *Life@Work* digital newsletter, tenth edition, March 2000. The Life@Work Co. copyright © 2000, www.lifeatwork.com. Reprinted by permission; quoted on page 67.

Tim and Jan Wright, eds.
Contemporary Worship, (Nashville: Abingdon Press, copyright © 1997). Used by permission; quoted on page 65.

Sources of Songs and Prayers

America
Excerpt from "Our Hearts," © 1993 Integrity's Hosanna! Music/ASCAP Integrity's Praise! Music/BMI. All rights reserved. International copyright secured. Used by permission c/o Integrity Music, Inc. 1000 Cody Road, Mobile, AL 36695; quoted on page 50.

Excerpt from prayer by Peter Marshall. Source: *Praise and Worship Study Bible,* (Wheaton: Tyndale House Publishers, Inc); quoted on page 70.

China
Author of prayer unknown. Source: *United Methodist Hymnal,* The United Methodist Publishing House, copyright © 1989 (Nashville: Abingdon Press). Used by permission; quoted on page 61.

Europe
Excerpt from song "Fairest Lord Jesus," author unknown, possibly written by Moravian Christians who fled Bohemia in the eighteenth century; quoted on page 85.

Germany
Excerpt from prayer by Martin Luther. Source: *Praise and Worship Study Bible,* (Wheaton: Tyndale House Publishers, Inc.); quoted on page 41.

Ghana
Author of Vagla song "Jesus Is The Way" unknown. Source: "'When I Heard These Songs, Tears Came to My Eyes:' The Vagla Scripture-Song Workshop," Paul Neeley, Sue Hall, Mary Hendershott, SIL, *Ethnomusicology News,* vol. 7, no. 1, p. 6. Used by permission; quoted on page 83.

Ireland
Prayer adapted from the *Prayer Book of the Church of Ireland,* excerpt. Source: *Praise and Worship Study Bible,* (Wheaton: Tyndale House Publishers, Inc.); quoted on page 87.

Japan
Excerpt from song "Here Oh Lord." Text by Tokuo Tamaguchi, © 1958, The United Methodist Publishing House (administered by The Copyright Company c/o The Copyright Company, Nashville, TN). All rights reserved. International copyright secured. Used by permission; quoted on page 84.

Kenya
Author of prayer unknown. Source: *United Methodist Hymnal,* The United Methodist Publishing House, copyright © 1989, (Nashville: Abingdon Press). Used by permission; quoted on page 40.

Malawi
Tumbuka song "Humbly in Your Sight." Text by Tom Colvin, copyright © 1976, Hope Publishing Co., Carol Stream, IL. All rights reserved. Used by permission; quoted on page 73.

New Hebrides
Author of prayer unknown. Source: *Chalice Hymnal,* Christian Board of Publication, (St. Louis, Chalice Press, copyright © 1995) Used by permission; quoted on page 74.

Papua New Guinea
Authors of Yawu songs "The Father's Word" and "Father God" unknown. Source: Helen Marten, 1999. Used by permission; quoted on page 39, 52.

Philippines
Excerpt from song "Blessed be God." Text by Salvador T. Martinez, copyright © 1989 by WGRG The Iona Community (Scotland). Used by permission of GIA Publications, Chicago, exclusive agent. All rights reserved. Used with permission; quoted on page 27.

Togo
Excerpt from Ife song "You Are God," author unknown. Source: "God's plan, power and praise among the Ife," Paul Neeley, (Dallas: SIL Ethnomusicology Department, 1998). Used by permission; quoted on page 45.

Photographers

Edgar Stephen Beach, page 56

Dan Bonnell, page 42

David Duncan, pages 20, 36

Craig Duddles, pages 12, 16, 17, 29, 31, 32, 34, 69, 74, 80, 81, 86

June Hathersmith, pages 24, 26, 28, 30, 46, 50, 58, 59, 62, 64, 65, 78, 80, 82, 84, 85

Robert Head, page 22

Don Hesse, pages 22, 35, 79

Becky Keller, page 72

Bob Mantell, pages 18, 19

Helen Marten, page 53

Rick McArthur, page 54

Brian Reese, page 20

Jim Rupp, page 21

Dean Schauer, pages 15, 17, 25, 35, 39, 41, 51, 81

Perry Schlie, pages 52, 55

Paul Smith, page 58

Hugh Steven, pages 37, 38

Johny Tenegra, page 41

John Walton, page 75